When Your World Shatters

Copyright © 2021 Ron Prosise

ISBN: 9798509523014

Scripture quotations are from the Christian Standard Bible®, Copyright © 2017 by Holman Bible Publishers. Used by permission.

 arrant Press

Sacramento, California

CONTENTS

Preface

This book came out of a time of great personal crisis and distress. I experienced many different emotions – shock, grief, instability, fear, and weakness. As a pastor and chaplain, I was much more confident on the other side, reaching out to people who were suffering. But now that I was going through a valley of deep darkness, I was overwhelmed with uncertainty and doubts.

There are strange paradoxes of suffering that can make this time even more difficult. You want to trust God, but you have doubts. You want to draw near to God, but you find it's hard to pray. You want help, but you are unsure of what that would be.

During this time, a tremendous help to me was the book of Psalms – the many cries and prayers of believers who also went through crisis, confusion, and anguish. What they wrote helped me to process and express my own difficult thoughts and feelings. Their examples also gave me direction for a way forward. The psalms do not give easy, matter-of-fact steps to recovery. No, they show people who are grappling with their affliction and pain – and finding hope in the Lord.

As you read through the psalms, you will encounter an interesting Hebrew word: *Selah*. Charles Spurgeon explains, "Selah… is a musical pause… wherever we see 'Selah,' we should look upon it as a note of observation. Let us read the passage which precedes and succeeds it with greater earnestness, for surely there is always something excellent where we are required to rest and pause and meditate."[1]

This book is designed to guide you to God in your pain. The prayers of the psalmists will help you express your thoughts and feelings to the Lord, finding in him the grace and hope you need. In each day's reading, you will see the focus is on one particular psalm, highlighting the emotions and experiences of those who have walked through painful times in positive ways. It's what the psalmist prayed in Psalm 119:76, *"May your faithful love comfort me as you promised your servant."* May this be true of you as well, and may you experience God's comforting, strengthening, protecting love as you draw near to him in your distress.

[1] C. H. Spurgeon, *The Treasury of David, Vol. I* (London: Passmore and Alabaster, 1870), 25

The Lord is near the brokenhearted...

Psalm 34:18

Shock

Psalm 143

"This can't be happening"

It was the news that you never could imagine getting. You still can't believe it, you still can't fathom what happened. You feel dazed. Your world has been shattered.

What do you do? How can you move forward?

Psalm 143 is a cry of someone well familiar with tragedy. David experienced extensive trauma throughout his life – the loss of his job, isolation, the threat of death, the abandonment of his wife, the death of his best friend, the rape of his daughter, and the murder of his children. It is not known which crisis led to this psalm, but consider his words:

Lord, hear my prayer. In your faithfulness listen to my plea, and in your righteousness answer me.

For the enemy has pursued me, crushing me to the ground, making me live in darkness like those long dead.

My spirit is weak within me; my heart is overcome with dismay.

I spread out my hands to you; I am like parched land before you. Selah (verses 1, 3-4, 6)

In vivid terms David speaks of what has happened to him. His life was crushed to the ground. The light has gone out in his world. His spirit is weak and his heart is overcome with dismay. So what does he do? In his distress, David prays:

Answer me quickly, Lord; my spirit fails. Don't hide your face from me, or I will be like those going down to the Pit. Let me experience your faithful love in the morning, for I trust in you. Reveal to me the way I should go because I appeal to you. (verses 7-8)

In his desperation, David turns to God. He cries out for help, asking the Lord to show him the way to move forward.

In his own shock in Gethsemane, God's son Jesus was "deeply distressed and troubled" (Mark 14:33). In that situation, he cried out to the Father. And in drawing near to God, Jesus found what he needed. Right now, whether you are overwhelmed with feelings or can't feel anything at all, cry out to the Lord. Pray through the words of this psalm and be reminded of God's great love for you. Draw near to him, asking for his help.

Anguish

Psalm 77

" I'm engulfed in painful thoughts and feelings"

The psalms are intimate glimpses of believers pouring out their hearts to God. Psalm 77 is one of those prayers of someone in anguish because of tragedy. Look at how he responds:

> *I cry aloud to God, aloud to God, and he will hear me.*
> *I sought the Lord in my day of trouble. My hands were continually lifted up all night long; I refused to be comforted.*
> *I think of God; I groan; I meditate; my spirit becomes weak.*
> *Selah You have kept me from closing my eyes; I am troubled and cannot speak.* (verses 1-4)

In his distress the psalmist Asaph turns to the Lord, crying out to him. But this does not immediately bring him relief and comfort. His thoughts only make him sink deeper in his anguish so that he cannot sleep; his trouble has strangled him so that he can't express it. So Asaph turns his thoughts to the good that God has done in the past:

> *I will remember the Lord's works; yes, I will remember your ancient wonders.*
>
> *I will reflect on all you have done and meditate on your actions.* (verses 11-12)

4

It can be difficult to receive comfort and encouragement from the Lord when all you feel is anguish. The truth is, God has been at work in your life in the past. He has given you promises of goodness for the present and hope for the future. Remembering this, as Asaph did, will bring encouragement in the Lord, the one who takes action when his people are in anguish:

> *You are the God who works wonders; you revealed your strength among the peoples. With power you redeemed your people.* (verses 14-15)

In these reminders, Asaph's perspective comes into a new focus, and he concludes his psalm speaking of God's faithfulness as a shepherd: *"You led your people like a flock"* (verse 20). Echoing this, Jesus speaks these words of compassion to you, *"My sheep hear my voice, I know them and they follow me"* (John 10:27). He is the good shepherd who will lead you through your anguish.

Consider all that God has done for you and has promised to do. Let those thoughts of his faithfulness encourage you to walk forward today.

Tears

Psalm 42

" I'm trying to process what has happened to me "

In Psalm 42, the psalmist begins his prayer using a vivid word picture to express his condition:

> *As a deer longs for flowing streams, so I long for you, God. I thirst for God, the living God. When can I come and appear before God? My tears have been my food day and night while all day long people say to me, "Where is your God?" I remember this as I pour out my heart: how I walked with many, leading the festive procession to the house of God, with joyful and thankful shouts.* (verses 1-4)

Peace and joy are gifts God gives to his children. But in times of distress, these gifts may seem only distant memories. The psalmist describes his condition as a thirst for God who is living water to his parched soul. Yet instead of this life-giving refreshment, the psalmist only tasted the bitter water of tears. But tears are an important part of processing through your pain. Jesus understands your distress – he experienced great anguish and cried out to God with tears: *"During his earthly life, he offered prayers and appeals with loud cries and tears to the one who was able to save him from death, and he was heard"* (Hebrews 5:7).

As his psalm continues, the psalmist responds in a very intriguing way. Instead of merely to listening to his soul with its thoughts and feelings of sorrow, he begins speaking to his soul:

> *Why, my soul, are you so dejected? Why are you in such turmoil? Put your hope in God, for I will still praise him, my Savior and my God.* (verse 5)

This is the expression of a heart of faith. The psalmist tells his soul, *"Why are you acting this way? You need to put your hope in God, not circumstances or feelings. Listen soul, I am going to still praise the Lord, because he is my Savior, he will deliver me."* And as his soul again tries to assert its sorrowful thoughts and feelings, the psalmist once more takes charge and tells his soul what to do:

> *Why, my soul, are you so dejected? Why are you in such turmoil? Put your hope in God, for I will still praise him, my Savior and my God.* (verse 11).

Tears and sorrow are natural responses in a time of grief. Weep and pour your heart out to the Lord. Speak to your soul, directing it to trust the Lord in your turmoil.

Questions

Psalm 13

"Why is this happening? Where is God in this?"

As time goes on, unanswered questions can add to your distress. In Psalm 13, David brings his perplexing thoughts to the Lord:

> *How long, Lord? Will you forget me forever? How long will you hide your face from me?* (verse 1)

These are striking questions. It seemed to David (and can appear to you) that the Lord doesn't care about him and what he was going through, that God had forgotten him. But instead of replaying those thoughts in his mind, David brings them to the Lord, crying out to him in his prayer.

> *How long will I store up anxious concerns within me, agony in my mind every day? How long will my enemy dominate me?* (verse 2)

The Lord was not offended by David's thoughts and questions. We know this because this psalm is in God's word as an example and guide to us. Rather than remain at a distance, the Lord encourages you to draw near and pour out your heart to him even with your confusion and questions.

David then transitions from honest questions to bold requests:

Consider me and answer, Lord my God. Restore brightness to my eyes; otherwise, I will sleep in death. My enemy will say, "I have triumphed over him," and my foes will rejoice because I am shaken. (verses 3-4)

David implores the Lord to consider him, answer him, and restore him. As David brings his questions and requests to the Lord, he focuses on God's faithfulness and goodness:

But I have trusted in your faithful love; my heart will rejoice in your deliverance. I will sing to the Lord because he has treated me generously. (verses 5-6)

David's confidence is in the Lord's faithful love, which gives him assurance of deliverance. Similarly, Jesus trusted the Father in his suffering: *"when he was insulted, he did not insult in return; when he suffered, he did not threaten but entrusted himself to the one who judges justly."* (1 Peter 2:23). While David might not be joyful as he prays his psalm, he believes that gladness will return and that he will sing again because of the Lord's goodness to him. Bring your own questions and requests to the Lord and trust in his faithful love.

Overwhelmed

Psalm 55

" I don't know what to think or feel..."

Going through a life-changing experience can be overwhelming. So many thoughts and feelings can swirl through your heart and mind like a whirlpool, dragging you further and further down.

Psalm 55 vividly expresses the feeling of being emotionally overwhelmed with anguish and fear:

> *My heart shudders within me; terrors of death sweep over me. Fear and trembling grip me; horror has overwhelmed me. I said, "If only I had wings like a dove! I would fly away and find rest. How far away I would flee; I would stay in the wilderness. Selah I would hurry to my shelter from the raging wind and the storm."* (verses 4-8)

In his distress, David feels overwhelmed, paralyzed physically and emotionally. He wonders how he can escape the trouble and pain. It can be tempting to seek relief by fleeing either physically or mentally with some distraction or way of numbing your mind. As appealing as this might be, it only brings temporary relief and can make your situation even worse.

David realizes that these escapes from the storm are mirages; the only true refuge is found in the Lord:

But I call to God, and the Lord will save me. I complain and groan morning, noon, and night, and he hears my voice. Cast your burden on the Lord, and he will sustain you; he will never allow the righteous to be shaken. (verses 16-17, 22)

Have you heard it said that the Lord will not give you more than you can handle? That is not true. Scripture testifies that the Lord will indeed give you more than you can handle, so that you will turn to him. Jesus was also overwhelmed when he said, *"I am deeply grieved to the point of death"* (Matthew 26:38-39). It was then that he sought the Father in prayer. This is what David does. He trusts that the Lord will hear his prayers and deliver him. Your burden is too heavy – the Lord is here for you cast it on him, trusting him to sustain you.

Express to God in prayer your desire to find refuge in him, casting your burden on the Lord, and trusting in his sustaining peace and strength.

Instability

Psalm 46

" My world has been shaken"

You were made to live in peace and stability. But trouble, catastrophe and ongoing pain can leave you shaken and unsettled. This instability can reveal where you have your confidence. It could be that your security is not in the Lord but in favorable circumstances. The problem with that is that circumstances change. And when disaster happens, it's like an earthquake shaking your world. That's when you need to hear what Psalm 46 is saying to you:

> *God is our refuge and strength, a helper who is always found in times of trouble. Therefore we will not be afraid, though the earth trembles and the mountains topple into the depths of the seas, though its water roars and foams and the mountains quake with its turmoil. Selah* (verses 1-3)

In times of instability, the Lord is near, he is "always found." This is the reason that, even in the midst of disruption and upheaval, the psalmist can confidently say, "We will not be afraid." The truth of God's nearness is repeated in the psalm:

> *The Lord of Armies is with us; the God of Jacob is our stronghold. Selah* (verse 7 and final verse 11)

The promise of God's nearness is fulfilled in Jesus, the one who came down from heaven. His name is Immanuel, which means, *"God is with us"* (Matthew 1:23).

This psalm, together with the rest of Scripture, emphasizes that God is very near. He is with you to give you the help you need. Draw near to him, your refuge and helper, and trust him for the stability and peace that he wants to give you.

God will help her when the morning dawns. (verse 5).

The beginning of every day brings you the promise of God's help.

The Lord says this, *"Be still, and know that I am God"* (verse 10). Be assured that in the instability of circumstances, thoughts and feelings, the Lord is God. He is with you and promises to be your stronghold and your refuge. Look to him for the peace and stability you need.

Fear

Psalm 23

" I am so afraid..."

As a shepherd, David was familiar with the many dangers that sheep face, including vicious predators and perilous terrain. Sheep need protection from these threats. They need a shepherd. So do you. Life in this broken world can be very dangerous and fearful. That's why David begins this psalm saying,

> *The Lord is my shepherd; I have what I need.* (verse 1)

Like sheep, people can become easily distressed. David experiences this, and so he looks to the Lord, his shepherd who knows what he needs. The Lord gives you rest and cares for you and he is carefully guiding you in the way you should go.

> *He lets me lie down in green pastures; he leads me beside quiet waters. He renews my life; he leads me along the right paths for his name's sake.* (verses 2-3)

The greatest calming influence is upon sheep is the presence of the shepherd. The same is true for believers:

> *Even when I go through the darkest valley, I fear no danger, for you are with me; your rod and your staff – they comfort me. You prepare a table before me in the presence of my enemies; you anoint my head with oil; my cup overflows.* (verses 4-5)

14

The dark valley is still there, but the promise you have is that your mighty, loving shepherd is with you. Did you notice that David said that the Lord is leading *through* the darkest valley? This is not your final stopping point. The Lord has a destination he is taking you, and you can trust his wisdom. He is intimately involved in your life, preparing a table for you.

Only goodness and faithful love will pursue me all the days of my life, and I will dwell in the house of the Lord as long as I live. (verse 6)

These are more than just encouraging thoughts in this psalm. Jesus came to fulfill these truths, saying, *"I am the good shepherd. The good shepherd lays down his life for the sheep"* (John 10:11). He gave up his life to bring you the goodness and love that continues to protect and to pursue you all the days of your life. When you are fearful, thank the Lord for his strong and loving presence. Ask that he would comfort you and calm your fears.

Alone

Psalm 22

" God seems so far away"

Someone has said, "Being alone is more painful than being hurt." But when you experience both together, the pain can seem unbearable. This was the situation of the psalmist when he cried out these distressing words:

My God, my God, why have you abandoned me? Why are you so far from my deliverance and from my words of groaning? (verse 1)

The psalmist tries to reconcile what he knows of God with what he is experiencing. If God promises to be near, why does he feel so alone? If God cares, why doesn't he help? The psalmist doesn't understand, so he cries out to the Lord. But there is no response – the psalmist still feels forsaken by God and by others:

Don't be far from me, because distress is near and there's no one to help. (verse 11)

What do you do when you feel alone, when the Lord seems far away, when you cry out to him and he does not answer? You may feel despairing and want to give up. You may feel that your prayers don't matter to God. You might look for relief and comfort elsewhere. But here we see the psalmist showing a better way as he cries out to the Lord:

But you, Lord, don't be far away. My strength, come quickly to help me. (verse 19)

This was Jesus' psalm; he prayed these words from the cross, crying out, *"My God, my God, why have you abandoned me?"* (Matthew 27:46). He didn't just feel abandoned by God; he was truly forsaken. He went through this to be your savior, so that you would never have to be alone, so that you could be reconciled and received by God as his child. Thank the Lord for this life-changing blessing!

For he has not despised or scorned the suffering of the afflicted one; he has not hidden his face from him but has listened to his cry for help. (verse 24).

David takes confidence that the Lord is with him and truly cares for him. When you feel alone, when you are unsure of God's presence, draw near to the Lord, trusting his promise to draw near to you (James 4:8).

Anger

" I get angry when I think about what happened"

Anger is a natural reaction for those who are suffering. But while anger may momentarily feel good, it will not bring you relief and might even lead you to sin. So what do you do with those feelings and thoughts? David shows us how to respond – crying out to the Lord:

Answer me when I call, God, who vindicates me. You freed me from affliction; be gracious to me and hear my prayer. (verse 1)

David remembers how the Lord delivered him from his suffering in the past. This gives him confidence that God will show his love in his present affliction. David then continues his prayer:

Be angry and do not sin… (verse 4)

Anger in itself is not sin – it's what is done with it that is crucial. Sometimes anger is felt right away. Other times anger surfaces later. But the question is, *Will you let your emotions take control?* The danger is where those emotions will take you. You can be angry at what others did to you, and that anger can lead to resentment, retaliation, and bitterness. You can be angry at yourself, and that anger can lead to regret, unrelieved guilt, and self-hatred. You can even become angry at God, leading to doubt and distancing yourself from the only one who can bring you healing and restoration. So consider what David says:

> ...*on your bed, reflect in your heart and be still.* *Selah*
> (verse 4)

That is good advice for when you are angry – to stop, to be still and reflect. It is important right now to control your emotions instead of being controlled by them. Realize what is going on inside you, and consider who God is in light of what you are going through – he is the one who knows your affliction and has promised to act. Reflect on who he is – faithful, wise and loving. Consider and claim what he promises – to draw near to you, to strengthen you and to give you peace.

Jesus also experienced anger (Mark 3:5). But he never let anger lead him to sin – he always manifested the fruit of the Spirit in self-control and did what was right for whatever situation he faced. Turn to the Lord for the help you need in your anger so that you also can respond in a right way.

Broken

Psalm 34

"What happened to me was devastating"

Tucked in the middle of this jubilant psalm is a reminder that being God's child does not mean you will not experience trouble:

One who is righteous has many adversities. (verse 19)

In the previous verse the psalmist uses this term to describe believers who have experienced severe adversity: *brokenhearted.* But this is actually beyond brokenhearted – the literal Hebrew word is *broken.* Afflictions may leave you broken. This brokenness can't be fixed by positive thinking, coping techniques, or a four-step plan to get you back on track. A broken person can be very discouraged or even despairing. That's why the psalmist says this:

The Lord is near the broken; he saves those crushed in spirit. (verse 18)

While it is true that severe adversity may leave you crushed and broken, that is not the only truth. The Lord has compassion, he is near. Jesus came to *"heal the broken"* (Isaiah 61:1). He did this by becoming broken himself, giving up his life on the cross. While restoration may seem very distant from you now, God has a good purpose for all you are suffering.

Yet as you continue reading, you may be perplexed by this verse:

He protects all his bones; not one of them is broken. (verse 20)

The same word for *broken* is used in verses 18 and 20. How can it be that God is close to the broken yet protects their bones from being broken? The picture is of someone physically wounded yet who has been protected from a more severe breaking of bones. So it is with you. You may experience very painful emotional wounds, but he will protect you from the more severe shattering of your soul. The Lord is indeed watching over you. And he has promised to be near to you and to protect you.

Jesus was pierced and crushed so that he could bring healing through his wounds (Isaiah 53:5). The gospel is the good news of a broken Savior offering compassion and grace. In your brokenness, you may find your own thoughts and feelings do not align with God's promises to you. If so, can you say, "Lord, help me believe *you* more than I believe *me*"?

Listen to the hopefulness of the psalmist's words: *"This poor man cried, and the Lord heard him and saved him from all his troubles"* (verse 6). In your brokenness, cry out to the Lord.

Shame

Psalm 69

" I feel humiliated..."

It might be something terrible that was done to you. It could be regret over something that you did. Was it some kind of attack or abuse? Rejection? Misunderstanding? Failure? Whatever the reason, you feel shame. David expresses it vividly:

Save me, God, for the water has risen to my neck. I have sunk in deep mud, and there is no footing; I have come into deep water, and a flood sweeps over me. (verses 1-2)

David vividly expresses his situation to God, that he is in distress with a flood that sweeps over him – he has no footing and he is drowning. His distress and his shame came because of others, *"my deceitful enemies, who would destroy me"* (verse 4). But he honestly admits that also he brought shame on himself:

God, you know my foolishness, and my guilty acts are not hidden from you. (verse 5).

These emotions can cause you to feel exposed. You wrestle with those awful thoughts and feelings, feeling rejected and unworthy. David describes it this way: *"shame has covered my face"* (verse 7). Shame had enveloped his life. He felt needy. But look what David did, in this word of encouragement for himself and for you:

You who seek God, take heart! For the Lord listens to the needy and does not despise his own who are prisoners. (verses 32-33).

The Lord is not far off and distant from you in what you are experiencing. Jesus understands your troubles because he experienced the fullness of suffering. *"He was despised and forsaken of men, a man of sorrows and acquainted with grief"* (Isaiah 53:3). And in Jesus' own shameful death *"he endured the cross, despising the shame"* (Hebrews 12:2). So whether it is shame from what someone did to you or regret because of what you did, Jesus bore your shame and overcame it. This means that God sees you clothed in the perfect righteousness of Christ, and you are more loved and accepted than you know.

This is why David says, *"take heart,"* because of all God has done for you in his love. In your shame and regret the Lord is listening to your expressions of pain and your cry for forgiveness. Draw near to him in prayer to receive his overcoming love.

Frustration

Psalm 131

"Why did this have to happen?"

As you deal with what has happened to you, frustrating thoughts can swirl around in your mind. It might seem that these thoughts are helping you deal with your crisis. But they can lead to further frustration. In Psalm 131, the psalmist shows a better way to deal with confusing thoughts and unanswered questions:

> *Lord, my heart is not proud; my eyes are not haughty. I do not get involved with things too great or too wondrous for me.*
> (verse 1)

In a time of crisis, you want to be in control, for life to go the way you would prefer. If you can't have that, you want at least to understand why. This leads to frustration. Wisdom realizes that God doesn't always give the reasons for what he has allowed in your life and faith rests in that. The psalmist says to God, "Lord, I'm letting go of trying to figure out things that are beyond my understanding."

> *Instead, I have calmed and quieted my soul like a weaned child with its mother; my soul is like a weaned child.*
> (verse 2)

When a hungry, nursing child is on his mother's lap, he is not at peace – he is frustrated and agitated. If he doesn't get what he wants, he fusses and cries. But when that same child is weaned, there is a dramatic change. There is no fretting, no agitation. The child is quiet and peaceful. He is content in the presence of the parent, not just what he wants the parent to give him.

Think of your own soul as a little child sitting on your lap. It can be frustrated, demanding, and agitated in its turmoil. Or you can direct your soul to quietness and rest in God's loving care.

Israel, put your hope in the Lord, both now and forever. (verse 3)

The writer of Hebrews encourages you to *"hold on to the courage and the confidence of our hope"* that you have in Jesus (Hebrews 3:6). Jesus is working in ways that are "too wondrous" for you to understand. Tell him that you want to trust him to bring you peace and confident hope.

Weakness

Psalm 102

" I used to be strong, but now I feel so weak"

The inspired title of Psalm 102 is *"A prayer of a suffering person who is weak and pours out his lament before the Lord."* Suffering can take a physical and emotional toll. And when that happens, it becomes even more difficult to endure hardship. It is hard to find yourself in a situation where, because of distress, you are not strong and capable – you are weak. When you are weak it can be difficult to try to do things that need to be accomplished, to fulfill your responsibilities, to keep going.

In his suffering and weakness, the psalmist cries out to the Lord:

> *Lord, hear my prayer; let my cry for help come before you...*
> *My heart is suffering, withered like grass.* (verses 1, 4)

Instead of trying to bolster himself in his own strength, the psalmist admits his weakness and draws near to God. His prayer reveals many dimensions of suffering including physical wasting (verse 3), lack of appetite (verse 4), isolation (verse 6), sleeplessness (verse 7), rejection (verse 8), and uncontrollable weeping (verse 9). The psalmist feels like a condemned prisoner (verse 20). And yet, he realizes that what has happened to him is more than mere happenstance. The Lord has made him weak:

He has broken my strength in midcourse; he has shortened my days. (verse 23).

This seems inexplicable – why would the Lord break the strength of his child? There is an important reason the Lord allows weakness – so that his child would grow closer to him and experience the greater power of God. Jesus had to remind his apostle of this, saying, *"My grace is sufficient for you, for my power is perfected in weakness"* (2 Corinthians 12:9). The Lord will allow you to become weak so that you might become even stronger in his might.

The psalmist felt that his situation was a prison and he prayed to be freed. Sometimes God will deliver you from the threat. Other times he will use that prison to show you important truths, to accomplish something good in you. And so, your weakness is God's opportunity to show his strength in your life.

Jesus said, *"the Son is not able to do anything on his own"* (John 5:19). The Lord gave up the power he had in heaven to live a life of weakness on earth – experiencing hunger, thirst, exhaustion, poverty, temptation, and suffering. Tell Jesus what you are going through and be assured that he understands and is ready to strengthen you so that you too can say, *"When I am weak, then I am strong"* (2 Corinthians 12:10).

Bitterness

Psalm 73

" What happened was so wrong "

In dealing with the aftermath of your tragedy, thoughts will swirl around in your mind. It's easy to look around and compare your life to others. As the psalmist did exactly this, it tempted him with bitter thoughts:

> *For I envied the arrogant; I saw the prosperity of the wicked. They have an easy time until they die... They are not in trouble like others...* (verses 3-5)

Why does God make life so hard for his own and seem to give the wicked a pass? This is baffling.

> *Did I purify my heart and wash my hands in innocence for nothing? For I am afflicted all day long...* (verses 13-14)

Why does God treat his own this way? It might seem that people who don't care about God have it better. What is the point of obeying God? These thoughts were leading the psalmist toward becoming bitter: *"When I became embittered and my innermost being was wounded, I was stupid and didn't understand"* (verses 21-22). But the Lord gave him a right perspective to help him understand:

> *Then I understood their destiny... They come to an end, swept away by terrors. Yet I am always with you; you hold my right hand. You guide me with your counsel, and afterward you will take me up in glory.* (verses 17-24)

28

The psalmist realizes that the wicked may momentarily seem to be doing well, but that is far outweighed by all that he has been given. He has a covenant relationship with God – his presence and help now, and the eternal, unshakeable hope of heaven. And in light of this he could say, *"I desire nothing on earth but you"* (verse 25).

How is it possible to live a life free from the bitterness and its destructive effects? Look at what 1 Peter 2:21-23 says: *"Christ also suffered for you, leaving you an example, that you should follow in his steps. He did not commit sin, and no deceit was found in his mouth; when he was insulted, he did not insult in return; when he suffered, he did not threaten but entrusted himself to the one who judges justly."* Follow Jesus in his example of trusting the Father in bitter circumstances, realizing you have so many blessings in your relationship with God.

Stuck

Psalm 40

" I feel trapped... I don't know what to do"

I waited patiently for the Lord, and he turned to me and heard my cry for help. He brought me up from a desolate pit, out of the muddy clay, and set my feet on a rock, making my steps secure. (verses 1-2)

What was David's situation in this psalm? He doesn't say, but there are many slimy pits in life: the pit of sin, the pit of bad circumstances, and the pit of defeat. When you are in one of these pits, you may feel helpless and stuck. In those times you need to do what David does: cry out to the Lord and wait patiently for him. Waiting is not just about what God will do at the end of the wait, but about what God wants to do during the wait. He wants to strengthen your faith, to deepen your relationship with him, to transform you into the likeness of his Son.

Lord, you do not withhold your compassion from me. Your constant love and truth will always guard me. (verse 11)

Stuck in a pit, you might lose sight of God's love. It can be easy to forget that he has a good purpose for what you are going through. Whatever pit you are in, the Lord wants you to remember his compassion, to draw near to him, to trust his love.

How happy is anyone who has put his trust in the Lord and has not turned to the proud or to those who run after lies! (verse 4)

David identifies different responses to being in a pit. One is to turn to the proud – yourself or someone else to try to bring freedom. Another is to run after lies, illusions that promise deliverance. But freedom only comes to those who place their trust in the Lord (verse 2). And with God's deliverance comes joy.

He put a new song in my mouth, a hymn of praise to our God. (verse 3)

The newness of this song is not *chronological* but *categorical*. It is not new by being recent, but it is new in that it is unlike any other. It is a new song of deliverance even as you wait, it is a song of worship, a song of joy. It is the song of freedom of those whose trust is in the Lord.

Hebrews 10:5-7 quotes this psalm, showing how David's greater Son Jesus fulfilled it. He says to the Father, *"I have come to do your will, God."* Ask Jesus for his help and joy to do God's will in waiting patiently when you feel stuck.

Faith

Psalm 28

"This ordeal has shaken my faith"

In the opening words of Psalm 28, the psalmist prays in what might seem to be a surprising way – with words that appear uncertain rather than confident:

> *Lord, I call to you; my rock, do not be deaf to me. If you remain silent to me, I will be like those going down to the Pit. Listen to the sound of my pleading when I cry to you for help, when I lift up my hands toward your holy sanctuary.* (verses 1-2)

Distress can challenge and even shake your faith. Like the psalmist, your prayers can feel more uncertain than confident. But as you look at this and other psalms, you will notice something – those in distress don't merely cry out in pain. No, they cry out to the God who cares, the God who hears, the God who helps. This is an act of faith. And in this faith, the psalmist makes this statement:

> *Blessed be the Lord, for he has heard the sound of my pleading.* (verse 6)

How did the psalmist know that the Lord heard his prayer? Through the pain and tears he understood God's character and trusted him. His faith may have been weak, but it was placed in the Lord, and God was pleased with that.

The Lord is my strength and my shield; my heart trusts in him, and I am helped. Therefore my heart celebrates, and I give thanks to him with my song. (verse 7)

Your faith may be weak, but like the psalmist, trust the Lord to help you. He is your strength and shield right now. Your faith may be small, but Jesus taught that the issue isn't how much faith you have, but where that faith is placed. He said, *"For truly I tell you, if you have faith the size of a mustard seed, you will tell this mountain, 'Move from here to there,' and it will move. Nothing will be impossible for you"* (Matthew 17:20). God's promises are for the weak, who feel their faith is small and that things are impossible. Even if it is weak, your faith is pleasing to the Lord.

Every promise of God – his peace, his strength, his wisdom, his hope – is yours even if your faith is small and weak. Like the rest of Scripture, Psalm 28 is a gift from God to you. Read the psalm again to assure your heart that the Lord is listening to you, encouraging your soul and strengthening your faith.

Caution

Psalm 141

"What other dangers are out there?"

Tragedy can make you feel as if there is a dark cloud surrounding you. You feel upset about what has happened and apprehensive about what else may come. In this psalm, David prays words that express the urgency of his distress.

Lord, I call on you; hurry to help me. Listen to my voice when I call on you. May my prayer be set before you as incense, the raising of my hands as the evening offering. (verses 1-2)

David asks that the Lord would hear him, that his prayer would be pleasing to the Lord, ascending as an offering of worship. But as he considers the way forward, David identifies a danger that may not be obvious to many who are suffering:

Lord, set up a guard for my mouth; keep watch at the door of my lips. (verse 3)

David is cautious, realizing he will be tempted to respond in ways that would not be good. Specifically, he is concerned about words that would express the turmoil of his heart. What are those temptations? There are many: words of complaint, anger, bitterness, gossip, and self-pity. David realizes that giving in to any of these temptations, even if he felt justified, he would be sinning against God. And sin would compound his difficult situation, making it

34

even more challenging. This is why David prays:

> *Do not let my heart turn to any evil thing or perform wicked acts with men who commit sin. Do not let me feast on their delicacies.* (verse 4)

Any of these temptations can seem justified when you are suffering. Acting on them can momentarily feel good, like David says, "feasting on delicacies." But these temptations are dangers and giving into them will make your circumstances worse. Remember that the Lord will lead you in a better way, a way of peace and goodness.

Because Jesus suffered *"when he was tempted, he is able to help those who are tempted"* (Hebrews 2:18). Thank the Lord for his help and pray that he would give you the wisdom for your temptations and the help that you need in this vulnerable time. And when you do stumble, remember that he is ready to forgive and restore you. In all of this, fix your eyes on Jesus as you pray with David, *"But my eyes look to you, Lord, my Lord"* (verse 8).

Refuge

Psalm 31

" I am so unsettled with all that has happened"

In times of distress, you can feel vulnerable and out of sorts. There is a great need to return to safety and stability. But how? This is on David's mind as he begins his prayer in Psalm 31:

Lord, I seek refuge in you; let me never be disgraced. (verse 1)

David understands that he cannot have stability and rest without security, and he realizes that this is only found in the Lord. That is why he prays:

Listen closely to me; rescue me quickly. be a rock of refuge for me, a mountain fortress to save me. For you are my rock and my fortress; you lead and guide me for your name's sake. You will free me from the net that is secretly set for me, for you are my refuge. (verses 2-4)

For David, the thought of God as refuge is not theoretical but very practical. He trusts the Lord's faithfulness to lead him through all the uncertainties and dangers in life. David expresses his confidence that that the Lord will deliver him from the traps that could ensnare him. What might those traps be? For David, it was enemies plotting to take his life. For you, it might be a very different yet dangerous trap: discouragement, anger, self-pity, resentment, bitterness, or hopelessness. Each of these is a threat with the power to defeat you and keep you ensnared. You need a refuge.

In light of these traps, David prays, *"Into your hand I entrust my spirit"* (verse 5). This actually became a bedtime prayer used by Jewish children in Bible times. As Jewish children went to sleep, they would recite, *"Into your hand I entrust my spirit,"* a prayer of childlike trust and assurance.

Jesus spoke this prayer when he was on the cross, in the midst of unimaginable physical, emotional, and spiritual suffering (Luke 23:46). But Jesus expands the prayer by adding a word at the beginning – *"Father, into your hands I entrust my spirit."* And in Christ, you too can pray that same prayer in your suffering, calling out to the One who is your Father, drawing near, entrusting yourself to him as your refuge to experience his peace and rest.

David prays, *"Blessed be the Lord, for he has wondrously shown his faithful love to me in a city under siege"* (verse 21). As you are under siege by circumstances and even when your own feelings and thoughts seem to be attacking you, be assured that the Lord loves you in a faithful and wondrous way. He is your rock of refuge.

Perspective

Psalm 27

"The challenges that I'm facing seem too big..."

What is larger – a child's ball or the sun? That seems like a ridiculous question, right? But if you were to hold that ball close enough to your face, it would completely block out the sun from your sight. So while the sun is vastly bigger than the largest child's ball, the ball would *seem* much bigger to you, as your perspective is skewed.

This is the crucial issue of perspective. When you are in pain, many things can loom large. In this psalm, David recounts many threats that he faced:

> *When evildoers came against me...* (verse 2)

> *...though a war breaks out against me...* (verse 3)

> *... adversity...* (verse 5)

> *... false witnesses rise up against me...* (verse 12)

Your troubles are different, but like David's, they are threatening. In the midst of all this, David says to God:

> *The Lord is my light and my salvation – whom should I fear? The Lord is the stronghold of my life – whom should I dread?* (verse 1)

Rather than fixating on threats and uncertainties, David turns his focus to the one who is bigger, the one who is his light, his salvation and his stronghold. And this perspective gives him the confidence he needs.

> *I am certain that I will see the Lord's goodness in the land of the living. Wait for the Lord; be strong, and let your heart be courageous. Wait for the Lord.* (verses 13-14)

Your life may be in pieces, but God wants to give you his goodness in Christ. Jesus not only lived out the truths of this psalm, he also enables you to live it out through his victory. He lived a perfect life, died a sacrificial death and then rose in triumph over every sin, every loss, every sorrow, every pain. He said, *"You will have suffering in this world. Be courageous! I have conquered the world"* (John 16:33). As you look to the Lord, let his supreme power and love be your perspective, giving you confidence and peace.

Waiting

Psalm 25

" I keep waiting for God to do something"

Waiting is challenging because we want to have control. If there is a problem in our lives, we want to fix it. If we can't fix it, we want God to take care of it – the sooner the better. And if the Lord doesn't work according to our timetable, it's hard to wait.

In Psalm 25 the psalmist finds himself helpless to fix his troubled circumstances. So he turns to the Lord in faith, praying:

> *Lord, I appeal to you. My God, I trust in you. Do not let me be disgraced; do not let my enemies gloat over me.* (verses 1-2)

Waiting is an opportunity to trust God, to see the Lord go beyond what you could do – not merely in fixing your situation but doing something better – accomplishing his good purpose in your life. The psalmist understood that, and so he says:

> *No one who waits for you will be disgraced.* (verse 3)

Once again the psalmist uses the word *disgraced,* which speaks of great disappointment and humiliation over painful circumstances. But the psalmist has confidence in the Lord's faithful love – he trusts that those who wait for God will not be disappointed. And the Lord not only has a purpose at the end of your waiting, he has a purpose for you *in* your waiting.

When his own brothers urged Jesus to take matters into his own hands, he replied, *"My time has not yet arrived"* (John 7:6). Jesus had confidence in the Father's purpose and timing for his life. But unlike Jesus, our difficulty is that God's ways are not our ways. Realizing this, the psalmist prays:

> *Make your ways known to me, Lord; teach me your paths.*
> *Guide me in your truth and teach me, for you are the God*
> *of my salvation; I wait for you all day long.* (verses 4-5)

The psalmist does more than passively wish for his circumstances to improve. He searches the wisdom of God's word, seeking and trusting the God who is his salvation, who graciously and powerfully rescues from the greatest danger of all: sin. If you trust him for that, you can trust him for every other danger and problem in your life. And one more all-important truth to hold onto – in your waiting, remember that you are not alone. Jesus has promised, *"I am with you always"* (Matthew 28:20).

Awareness

Psalm 103

" As I look around, all I see is bad"

In the midst of trouble, it's understandable that the bad would be at the forefront of your thoughts. And so you can easily lose sight of God's abundant blessings. The result is a diminished awareness, losing sight of all the good in your life. David gives a remedy for this, beginning with this encouragement:

> *My soul, bless the Lord, and all that is within me, bless his holy name. My soul, bless the Lord, and do not forget all his benefits.* (verses 1-2)

This awareness is a very helpful strategy. As mentioned earlier with Psalm 42, so often what we do is *listen to* our souls instead of *talking to* our souls. If your soul is feeling a certain way, it's easy to listen to it, to accept what it is saying, and allow yourself to follow that leading. If your soul is upset, it's easy to listen, accept that message, and continue to be upset. If your soul is angry, it's easy to listen, accept that message, and continue to be angry. If your soul is anxious or depressed, it's easy to listen, accept that message, and continue to be anxious or depressed. And so you are keenly aware of the negative message your soul is giving you and less aware of God's goodness.

Instead, David says, "Listen soul, here is what you are going to do. You are not going to fixate on the negative, forgetting all of the ways the Lord has shown you his love and his goodness. No, you are going to remember those blessings and live in joyful awareness of them, and be encouraged and uplifted."

Then David goes on to recount the many blessings the Lord has given him, letting this awareness bring gratitude and hope:

> *Who pardons all your iniquities, who heals all your diseases; Who redeems your life from the pit, who crowns you with lovingkindness and compassion; Who satisfies your years with good things, so that your youth is renewed like the eagle.* (verses 3-5).

So yes, you may have experienced great trouble, and your heart may be struggling with sorrow and fear. But be aware of God's nearness and goodness to you. Hear the words of Jesus: *"Don't be afraid, little flock, because your Father delights to give you the kingdom"* (Luke 12:32). In Christ, God has given you the riches of his kingdom: his forgiveness, goodness, love, and most of all, himself. Like David, tell your soul to thank the Lord, remembering all of his blessings.

Hope

Psalm 119

"Where do I go for help?"

In Psalm 119, the psalmist opens his heart to God, honestly expressing the painful realities of his situation in what is the longest of psalms. Consider a few of these vivid cries from his heart:

My life is down in the dust...

I am weary from grief...

Turn away the disgrace I dread...

I am severely afflicted...

Turn to me and be gracious to me...

Trouble and distress have overtaken me...

These are words of honest distress, the words of someone in need of hope. But what is striking is how each of his cries to the Lord ends. In every case, this suffering believer connects his affliction to the goodness and hope found in God's word:

My life is down in the dust; give me life through your word. (verse 25)

I am weary from grief; strengthen me through your word. (verse 28)

Turn away the disgrace I dread; indeed, your judgments are good. (verse 39)

I am severely afflicted; Lord, give me life according to your word. (verse 107)

Turn to me and be gracious to me, as is your practice toward those who love your name. (verse 132)

Trouble and distress have overtaken me, but your commands are my delight. (verse 143)

When Jesus asked his disciples if they were going to leave him as many others had done, Peter answered, *"Lord, to whom will we go? You have the words of eternal life"* (John 6:68). The psalms are Jesus' words of eternal life, helping you to connect your pain to God's goodness. He hears your cries and speaks to you his words of life and hope. Read through this entire psalm, underlining the verses that express your own distress and seeing how it can be connected to the Lord's goodness. Let your hope be renewed in the life-giving word of God.

Gratitude

Psalm 138

"It's hard to be thankful with what's happened"

In Psalm 138, the psalmist expresses gratitude to God:

I will give you thanks with all my heart. (verse 1)

We understand that gratitude is right, that we are to give thanks in all circumstances. But gratitude in the midst of painful circumstances can be very difficult. You might not be feeling thankful. You may have the perspective that you will thank God when your circumstances change or your prayers are answered. But consider what the psalmist says in the next verse:

I will bow down toward your holy temple and give thanks to your name. (verse 2)

When you give thanks, you immediately enter into God's presence. In your distress you might feel you are alone, left to deal with your situation by yourself. But the Lord is with you. This is a supreme reason for gratitude.

On the day I called, you answered me; you increased strength within me. (verse 3)

Being thankful does not mean denying reality or suppressing your feelings. The psalmist cried out to God when he was in need. What gratitude does is remind you of God's faithfulness in the past and his promises for the

46

present. Over and over in the gospels, Jesus expresses his gratitude to the Father, as in John 11:41 when he prayed, *"Father, I thank you that you heard me."* As you follow Christ's example of gratitude, your faith will be strengthened.

> *The Lord will fulfill his purpose for me. Lord, your faithful love endures forever; do not abandon the work of your hands.* (verse 8)

The psalmist concludes his prayer with confidence in God's faithful love. The Lord has a good purpose for you and he has promised to complete it. Express your gratitude to God, taking confidence in his love and his promises to you.

Peace

Psalm 85

" I can't seem to get settled"

In the loss and disruption of crisis, one of the greatest casualties is peace. The emotions of grief, uncertainty, anxiety, and fear can erode the tranquility in your life, leaving you feeling unsettled.

In Psalm 85 the psalmist begins with the truth that God has established the peace between himself and those who were in conflict with him because of sin:

> *You forgave your people's guilt; you covered all their sin. Selah* (verse 2).

This is salvation, *positional peace*. Trusting the Lord for his forgiveness brings peace *with* God. Guilt and condemnation are gone – you are loved and accepted by the Lord. On this basis of positional peace, the psalmist pleads for *experiential peace*, which is the peace *of* God. In times of disruption it might seem that the Lord is distant, or that he is displeased with you, as the psalmist who expresses his unsettled feelings in verse 4, *"Return to us, God of our salvation, and abandon your displeasure with us."* But your relationship with Him has not changed, he is still *"God of our salvation."* But what if peace is lacking? Look at what the psalmist declares:

I will listen to what God will say; surely the Lord will declare peace to his people. (verse 8)

This is such good counsel, to listen to what God declares in his word. The Lord has so much to say for those who have ears to hear. Listen to him speaking to you in his word. Let his voice be predominant in your life, in your distress.

Righteousness and peace will embrace. (verse 10)

The psalmist says that peace is united with righteousness. This is seen in the cross, where the righteous demands of God for our sins were fulfilled so that the peace of God could be accomplished. Jesus says, *"Peace I leave with you. My peace I give to you. I do not give to you as the world gives. Don't let your heart be troubled or fearful"* (John 14:27). The Prince of Peace gives you both positional and experiential peace.

Thank God for the peace that is yours in Christ. Pray for ears to hear what the Lord says as he declares peace to you so that as you grow in your trust of God you will grow in peace.

Strength

Psalm 10

" Where can I find strength I need?"

One of the predominant refrains of our culture is, "You are strong! You can do it!" Yet life has a way of hitting us with the reality that this is not always true. Illness, conflict, and tragedy all take their toll on our bodies and souls. Despite our best efforts to put on a brave face and rise above these challenges, we are not as strong as we would like to be. This was the case for the psalmist, who, when he was oppressed, beaten down and helpless (verse 10), cried out to the Lord in prayer:

> *Rise up, Lord God! Lift up your hand. Do not forget the oppressed.* (verse 12)

What brought the psalmist confidence in his weakness? Certainly it was knowing that the Lord heard his cries and would act. But there is another reason for encouragement that the psalmist speaks of as he continues his prayer:

> *But you yourself have seen trouble and grief, observing it in order to take the matter into your hands.* (verse 14a)

The Lord wants you to understand that he has a purpose in your weakness. He sees your trouble and grief and he will take action. The Lord has allowed you to be weak so that you will turn to him for the strength and help you need, trusting his compassion and faithfulness:

The helpless one entrusts himself to you; you are a helper of the fatherless. (verse 14b)

In this world, children are the weakest of all, and a child without parents is the most helpless. Yet the Lord has compassion on them and on all who entrust themselves to him. Weakness has a way of humbling us. But in that humility comes greater strength, the strength that only God can give:

Lord, you have heard the desire of the humble; you will strengthen their hearts. (verse 17)

When Jesus came to earth, he experienced humility that he had never known and weakness that culminated in his suffering and death on the cross to accomplish salvation. God worked his power in the weakness of Christ *"by raising him from the dead and seating him at his right hand in the heavens"* (Ephesians 1:20). And the apostle prays that we would know that this same power *"toward us who believe, according to the mighty working of his strength"* (verse 19). Ask God to strengthen your heart, trusting, as the psalmist did, that the Lord *"will listen carefully"* (verse 17) and he will surely help and strengthen you in your weakness.

Goodness

Psalm 84

"How can anything good come out of this ordeal?"

In your affliction, it might not be in the forefront of your thoughts. But make no mistake – God's goodness is there in your life. The psalmist is aware of the goodness of God's gifts, and more than that – he is drawn to the goodness of God himself:

How lovely is your dwelling place, Lord of Armies. I long and yearn for the courts of the Lord; my heart and flesh cry out for the living God. (verses 1-2)

Above all else, the psalmist longed for the goodness God's presence. He expresses the blessing of those in ancient Israel making the pilgrimage to come before God in his temple:

Happy are the people whose strength is in you, whose hearts are set on pilgrimage. As they pass through the Valley of Baca, they make it a source of spring water. (verses 5-6)

For many in Israel, it was a long journey to the temple. When they reached the valley of Baca, they would face a problem: how to make it through this desolate valley with no water. There could be the temptation to give up, to turn back. But the psalmist says that they transform this difficulty into a blessing – they make it a source of spring water. How? By digging for it. And so, they brought not only life-giving goodness to themselves, but a blessing to others who were also traveling this difficult journey.

What if the Lord has more in mind for you than just getting through your adversity? He may have you be a blessing to others – even in your pain – to those who need life-giving refreshment.

Jesus is the supreme example of this. He blessed others in his adversity right up to the night before his crucifixion, caring for his disciples and then saying to them, *"I have given you an example, that you also should do just as I have done for you"* (John 13:15). You are able to follow Christ's example of blessing others because of God's blessing to you:

> *For the Lord God is a sun and shield. The Lord grants favor and honor; he does not withhold the good from those who live with integrity.* (verse 11)

God promises that he will not withhold goodness from you. Take heart in that promise; take heart in God's goodness. And pray that he will use your experience to bring a blessing of goodness to others.

Restoration

Psalm 107

"Will life ever be the same again?"

Give thanks to the Lord, for he is good; his faithful love endures forever. (verse 1)

The reason the psalmist begins his psalm with gratitude is that God brings restoration. This is vividly pictured throughout this psalm – those under oppression by an enemy are redeemed (verses 2-3), those who wander are given a home (verses 4-9), the imprisoned are freed (verses 10-16), the afflicted are healed (verses 17-22), and those in danger are rescued (verses 23-32).

In times of great loss, such restoration might seem impossible. But this is God's specialty – *"to do above and beyond all that we ask or think"* (Ephesians 3:20). The psalmist testifies to this:

But he lifts the needy out of their suffering and makes their families multiply like flocks. The upright see it and rejoice, and all injustice shuts its mouth. (verses 41-42)

If you read through this psalm, you will notice how all of the images are illustrations of a far greater spiritual restoration. The Lord gives salvation (verses 2-3), a home (verses 4-9), freedom (verses 10-16), healing (verses 17-22), and deliverance (verses 23-32). What you have lost in this life may not be restored. But – *and this is so important* – what he does promise to restore is *you.*

Jesus came to fulfill the prophecy to bring restoration to people, *"He will not break a bruised reed, and he will not put out a smoldering wick"* (Matthew 12:20). In that day, flutes were made out of reeds that became damaged after repeated use. Unable to make a melody, the shepherd would simply snap the bruised reed and throw it away. It had lost its usefulness, so it would be discarded. *Smoldering wick* refers to oil lamps that brought light to a home. If the wick burned low, it would sputter with a failing light, and so be extinguished and discarded.

The bruised reed and smoldering wick are pictures of people who are injured. Christ is not through with those in pain. The Lord's compassion for you never fails, his mercies for you are new every morning. He brings restoration, giving a song to those who are bruised and rekindling to those who are in need of grace.

So as the psalmist encourages, *"Let whoever is wise pay attention to these things and consider the Lord's acts of faithful love"* (verse 43). Consider and trust the Lord's faithful love to do his good work in your life, rekindling your light and restoring your song.

Confidence

Psalm 66

" I want to trust God to work in this adversity"

Psalm 66 begins with the psalmist praising God:

Let the whole earth shout joyfully to God! Sing about the glory of his name; make his praise glorious. (verses 1-2)

What is the reason for such exuberant confidence? The psalmist is rejoicing over God's works because they are "awe-inspiring" (verse 3). He says, "Come and see the wonders of God" (verse 5). Look at how the psalmist explains God's awesome works:

For you, God, tested us; you refined us as silver is refined. You lured us into a trap; you placed burdens on our backs. You let men ride over our heads; we went through fire and water, but you brought us out to abundance. (verses 10-12)

God has a very good purpose for you in mind. A careful craftsman knows that silver is far more precious when it is refined. Similarly, the Lord only allows testing and trials because he knows the outcome. Although you can't see it at the time, God knows the blessings that will come from your suffering. So while you aren't able to have full understanding in God's ways, you can have confidence in his character, as the psalmist does:

Blessed be God! He has not turned away my prayer or turned his faithful love from me. (verse 20)

As you go through *"fire and water"* (verse 12), you may wonder why the Lord is allowing this in your life. But even though you can't see all the good things God will do through your affliction, you can have confidence in his faithful love to you.

The Lord does not delight in your suffering, but he is with you. When Christ was with Mary and Martha in their grief over the death of their brother Lazarus, the apostle records, *"Jesus wept"* (John 11:35). So it is with you – realize that Lord is moved with compassion in your suffering. And his compassion should give you confidence. The Lord cares about you and he is carefully orchestrating your life to accomplish his good purpose for you. That includes all aspects of life, even your suffering. His purpose for you is not a detached, remote abstraction. No, he is intimately involved in your life. Ponder these encouraging truths and ask the Lord to strengthen your confidence in him through this time of testing.

Joy

Psalm 126

" Will joy return to my life?"

Psalm 126 was written by another unknown believer who experienced great adversities. The affliction of those taken into captivity was great – the conquering of their country, the loss of their homes and livelihood, and the uprooting to a foreign land. This was a time of sorrow and tears. And then, remarkably, something happened:

> *When the Lord restored the fortunes of Zion, we were like those who dream. Our mouths were filled with laughter then, and our tongues with shouts of joy. Then they said among the nations, "The Lord has done great things for them." The Lord had done great things for us; we were joyful.*
> (verses 1-3)

Joy and even laughter came in a wonderful way after a long period of sorrow. It was obvious to them and to those looking on that the Lord had done this great work. But in the midst of gladness there is the realization that life would still be challenging:

> *Restore our fortunes, Lord, like watercourses in the Negev.*
> (verse 4)

The joy of freedom is mingled with the reality of the situation. After seventy years of the land being neglected, it would be very difficult to eke out an existence. The psalmist likens the situation to the Negev desert needing life-giving water. So the psalmist turns to God, praying for the Lord to restore what was lost. And what gives him encouragement is this truth:

Those who sow in tears will reap with shouts of joy. (verse 5)

The harvest only comes after a time of labor. The Lord does give the harvest, but it requires plowing, planting, watering, and weeding. And after all that hard work, there is the waiting. Though the tearful labor is hard – with tears, the promise of the harvest is joy.

Hebrews 12:2 speaks of Jesus facing the most difficult ordeal of his life and tells us to look to his example: *"For the joy that lay before him, he endured the cross, despising the shame, and sat down at the right hand of the throne of God."* Part of what allowed Jesus to go through unimaginable suffering was the joy that was ahead.

You may have to wait for joy, like the Israelites in captivity and Jesus in his agony. It may be difficult to even imagine joy coming back into your life. But like Jesus, there is joy set before you. Express to the Lord your desire to trust him for that.

Forward

Psalm 90

"What does the Lord have ahead for me?"

The author of Psalm 90, Moses, had many homes in his life – with his family, in a basket on the river, an Egyptian palace, the foreign country of Midian, and then in the wilderness. The journey of his life took many turns. So it is striking the way Moses begins his psalm:

> *Lord, you have been our refuge in every generation.*
> (verse 1)

Like Moses, the Lord is your true security amidst the instability of life. God is the One who never changes, never collapses, never fails. And that brings confidence. Moses continues in his psalm to consider how life is so fragile and fleeting. He says our days are *"struggle and sorrow"* (verse 10), and he asks three requests of God:

> *Teach us to number our days carefully so that we may develop wisdom in our hearts.* (verse 12)

Moses first asks to understand the brevity of life to be able to make the most of the time that God has given. This is foundational, a prayer for wisdom, for a right perspective of life, to trust in the Lord and not rely on your own understanding. He then goes on to ask another request of God:

Turn and have compassion on your servants. Satisfy us in the morning with your faithful love so that we may shout with joy and be glad all our days. Make us rejoice for as many days as you have humbled us, for as many years as we have seen adversity. (verses 13-15)

People say, "Time heals all wounds," but is that true? With the passing of time there may be a lessening of the pain, but only God is able to exchange sorrow for joy. That might seem impossible, which is why Moses prays, *"Let your work be seen by your servants"* (verse 16). He looks to the only one who can exchange sorrow for joy, the only one who can help him move forward. Then he asks one more request:

Let the favor of the Lord our God be on us; establish for us the work of our hands — establish the work of our hands! (verse 17)

Because of Jesus, God's favor *is* upon you. God's word says this about Jesus, *"Indeed, we have all received grace upon grace from his fullness"* (John 1:16). You can move forward with confidence because the Lord is with you and his grace is upon you. Look to him for all your need — peace, wisdom and strength — as the Lord is there to help you on your journey.

Assurance

Psalm 139

"Some days I'm still not so sure..."

The format of this book is not meant to give the impression that healing and restoration is a simple, straightforward process. At times in my own journey it appeared to be two steps forward and then one step back. Some days it seemed I had lost all the progress I had made. Even after writing this, at times I realized I was again dealing with reoccurring issues of anguish, instability, brokenness, doubts and weakness. So I would return to the particular psalm for whatever issue I was dealing with that day. And I would again discover the wisdom and encouragement from God that I needed.

In Psalm 139, David again finds assurance – not in his own strength, but in God. His eyes are lifted above the challenges and trials of his life to the Lord's marvelous care over him.

Lord, you have searched me and known me. You know when I sit down and when I stand up; you understand my thoughts from far away. You observe my travels and my rest; you are aware of all my ways. (verses 1-2)

David was confident that the Lord had a good purpose for him. This is the assurance that God wants you to have as well, that your life is designed by the wise and loving Creator. The events of your life are not without purpose:

...all my days were written in your book and planned before a single one of them began. (verse 16)

Your life – every one of your days – is carefully orchestrated by God to accomplish his good purpose for you. He is intimately involved in your life, as the psalmist declares:

You have encircled me; you have placed your hand on me. (verse 5)

Read verse 5 again. Do you realize what this is saying? God is with you, he has encircled you with his love, placing his strong, caring hand upon you. This is the assurance that you need – the love the Lord has for you, the love Jesus spoke of when he said, *"As the Father has loved me, I have also loved you. Remain in my love"* (John 15:9). The Lord has encircled you with his presence and love; he has placed his hand on you. May that truth be your assurance and joy right now in all that you are going through and in all the days of your life.

ABOUT THE AUTHORS

Ron and Donna Prosise have served in ministry together for over twenty-five years – Ron as a pastor and military chaplain, and Donna as a discipler of women. It was out of these experiences that this book was born. Through many interactions with people and their difficulties in this fallen world, they realized the greatest need in pain is to cry out to God and draw near to him through Jesus.

A Spanish version is available: *Cuando Tu Mundo Se Rompe*

Made in the USA
Las Vegas, NV
25 October 2021